Sanctuary

Also by Adrienne Su:

Middle Kingdom

Sanctuary

Adrienne Su

Manic D Press
San Francisco

Grateful acknowledgment is made to the following publications in which some of these poems originally appeared, some in slightly different form: *The Clarion Review, Crab Orchard Review, Eclipse, Electronic Poetry Review, Free Verse, Gargoyle, Greensboro Review, Hunger Mountain, Indiana Review, Literature and Belief, Meridians, MiPoesias, New Letters, Prairie Schooner,* and *Washington Square.*

And thanks to the editors of the following anthologies in which some of these poems were included: *Best American Poetry 2000* (Scribner); *Pushcart Prize XXIV* (Norton); *New American Poets: A Bread Loaf Anthology* (University Press of New England); *Asian American Poetry: The Next Generation* (University of Illinois Press); and *Poetry 30: Thirtysomething American Thirtysomething Poets* (Mammoth Books).

Cover design: Scott Idleman/BLINK

Library of Congress Cataloging-in-Publication Data

Su, Adrienne, 1967-
 Sanctuary / Adrienne Su.
   p. cm.
Summary: "Poems reflecting the myriad experiences of an Asian-American writer as a working mother and a child of immigrants, and the challenges that accompany these experiences"--Provided by publisher.
 ISBN-13: 978-1-933149-06-6 (trade pbk. original : alk. paper)
 ISBN-10: 1-933149-06-X (trade pbk. original : alk. paper)
 I. Title.
 PS3569.U13S36 2006
 811'.54--dc22

                    2006006476

For Aisling and Dervla

Contents

The English Canon

It's not that the first speakers left out women
Unless they were goddesses, harlots, or impossible loves
Seen from afar, often while bathing,

And it's not that the only parts my grandfathers could have played
Were as extras in Xanadu,
Nor that it gives no instructions for shopping or cooking.

The trouble is, I've spent my life
Getting over the lyrics
That taught me to brush my hair till it's gleaming,

Stay slim, dress tastefully, and not speak of sex,
Death, violence, or the desire for any of them,
And to let men do the talking and warring

And bringing of the news. I know a girl's got to protest
These days, but she also has to make money
And do her share of journalism and combat,

And she has to know from the gut whom to trust,
Because what do her teachers know, living in books,
And what does she know, starting from scratch?

Escape from the Old Country

I never had to make one,
no sickening weeks by ocean,

no waiting for the aerogrammes
that gradually ceased to come.

Spent the babysitting money
on novels, shoes, and movies,

yet the neighborhood stayed empty.
It had nothing to do with a journey

not undertaken, nor with dialect,
nor with a land that waited

to be rediscovered, then rejected.
As acid rain collected

above the suburban hills, I tried
to imagine being nothing, tried

to be able to claim, "I have
no culture," and be believed.

Yet the land occupies the person
even as the semblance of freedom

invites a kind of recklessness.
Tradition, unobserved, unasked,

hangs on tight; ancestors roam
into reverie, interfering at the most

awkward moments, first flirtations,
in doorways and dressing rooms—

But of course. Here in America,
no one escapes. In the end, each traveler

returns to the town where, everyone
knew, she hadn't even been born.

New York

In the beginning I was living hand to mouth,
footloose in the city that broke my heart.
You could say I had my head in the clouds,
but I also had sand in my craw. I was smart
enough to follow my nose—even if it went
the way of all flesh—but spurned the men
of learning who could have helped prevent
a hundred weeks of rain and sorrow. Back then
I thought there were dues to pay, an extra mile
a girl would have to go. Cold, wet to the skin,
I found my oracle in Chinatown. She smiled
and said, "Don't wear heart on sleeve." Didn't
mention death or taxes, art or life, love or money.
Before I could blink, she was showing me down
the steps to a street awash in milk and honey.
I could not speak. My heart was in my mouth.

Fear of Flying

They're sure of it: by hugging the ground
they will avert the day it swallows them.
As children, they were never thrilled

by the ungainly cart of cans and spoons,
the miniature lasagna and squares of cake.
When the oxygen masks dropped down

in the safety video, they heard a voice
instructing their parents: "Put a mask
on yourself before assisting those

who will never get over the sight
of a city through a film of cloud-matter
and the knowledge that their flight

was engineered by an imperfect species,
able only to fasten their seat belts
and pray to a deity in whom their belief

is as frail as their comprehension
of the forces that keep us aloft. Come
to think of it, don't bother to assist them."

On earth, with books, they're equally diffident.
Oddly, they favor airport reading. Books
with unhappy endings (say, *Oedipus Rex*) awaken

only righteous frustration: It was all his fault!
He should have sworn off sex and death—
he should have stayed home and not gone out

for anything, not to send a package or order
a pizza, or whatever they ate in those days,
to avoid the likelihood of running his father

down by mistake on the road to the pizzeria,
where some spectacular, lonely female
might be waiting to seduce him (Jocasta

could *cook*) with a primitive version
of, say, the Margherita—basil, tomatoes,
and mozzarella on a round of bread so thin

he wouldn't know it was leavened,
just as he wouldn't know, from any amount
of experience, that this was the woman.

Men at Forty

after Donald Justice

First they were our fathers and the fathers of our friends.
They drove us to school, checked on us at night,
And gave advice on pesky boys and science assignments.

Then they were our youngest uncles, our oldest cousins.
Although they had left the realm of the elders,
They were still more old than young, with jobs and children.

Then, overnight, they ceased to be family.
They greeted us differently, not mentioning our height,
Nor offering their hands, nor looking at us directly.

We didn't know why until we were twentyish
When one of them got too close and we cared no more
How many others he had, or what he had mortgaged,

But the bewitchment lasted only as long as the inequality.
When we got realistic and dissolved the obviously
Impossible compact, they were the more unhappy.

Now they're all around us, mostly wedded, some still adrift.
Many are somebody's father but not, to us, paternal.
Much like ourselves, they are a past with a future in it.

We can't remember what it was to love a boy of seventeen,
As if nothing would ever again be worthy,
Or what made anyone remarkable before this evening,

On which they are perfect in their ambivalence, exactly
What we always wanted, humbled, practically mortal,
Half ours and half nobody's, closing doors softly.

Women

It often means ourselves, undivided
army on this side of the wall,
trading hairbrushes, sworn to the death.

Other times, it's simply an utterance
to evoke the masculine condition:

a curse, murmured in italics,
sigh of loving exasperation,
an enemy in aggregate, a passion.

With children, it might mean liability,
commodity, boatload of victims.

Some hear it as conspiracy,
every girl out to get them,
cut off their fingers.

It's what others yet
believe they want, until they get it.

To one of us, a woman's the dearest friend,
bitterest rival. In the end, we'll be left
to hold all the conversation,

which is what the shopping readies us for;
the merchandise is secondary.

In the Maternity Shop

Just when we feel least like ourselves,
our selves are remade in the image
of fourth graders, as if what we did to get here

took place in immaculate ignorance,
as if our impulses were for dandelion-picking
or the purchase of lace for a sunbonnet.

Look at us: We were never in charge of anything.
We never threw away a packet of pills
or knowingly accepted an invitation

from a stranger who had no references.
All our early crushes were on movie stars.
When one day out of ether we got married,

we blithely accepted the symbolism
of the dress, on which we spent the money
some other woman might have spent on books

or airfare, then discovered conjugal life.
Although our wardrobes spent some months
providing for neither schoolgirl nor matriarch,

it wasn't long enough to be worth
an overhaul, so we went from giggling
to cooing in the same forgiving overdress,

which concealed a shape that was prenatal
until the day it was postnatal, the shape
of one for whom to give life is to live it.

Bargain

At first there is nothing but glamour in tragedy,
Daily life being forgettable unless it hurts.
Then comes deliberate spurning of luxury,
Less the pursuit of pain than of mild discomfort.

Next, the sense of travel gives way to place,
Just as one's beginnings conclude without warning
And lead to the formal making of a deal: the trade
Of what looks like less punishment for what looks like less living.

Wedding Gifts

Everywhere, a reason for caution:
crystal bowls, white teacups, porcelain.

Objects, which used to tumble in
on their way to the junk heap,
now possessed origins.

I had no idea what to do with a dog
that didn't come from the pound,

and now, as if suddenly old,
found frailties in places I never knew existed.
Casseroles leapt, glasses imploded—

I wept each time. I knew from poetry
that no one conquers entropy,

but I also knew from poetry
everyone has to try. Rescued, the animal
loses all anonymity

in a syllable, and the hero's nobility
dissolves into family.

Marriage is the same, with dishes and rings.
Vows or no vows, you embrace your own death,
journeying to which, you only get clumsier, and things,

which you thought mere material,
become irreplaceable.

Summer of the Abducted Child

That dry season, heavy on the hands,
our daughter edged toward two. It felt far
away from seven, Danielle van Dam's
final age, but it didn't feel far

from five, Samantha Runnion's.
Highways and suburbs grew vast
and sinister. Watching Erin Runnion
watch her daughter's casket

being carried away, I knew
what I was being made to feel
but let it happen; just as the news
could make your living room feel

like a sex offender's playground,
so could it make a public park
look like sanctuary. I found
myself hoping they'd cut out the hearts

of the murderers, despite what I knew
and believed. Asked what should happen,
Erin stated plainly, "I want him to undo
what he did," and the whole nation

became an underworld above which
wildflowers blossomed cruelly.
August brought the proper verdict
for the killer of Danielle, but *happily*

doesn't describe the way we cheered.
Our deities had revealed themselves
to be incompetent; all who appeared
to us in dreams were disheveled

kindergarten girls, whose messages
we couldn't understand. I had meant
to show my daughter the blessings
of the favored season, to plant

lettuces, basil, and sunflowers,
to feast on melons that cracked
at the touch of a blade, but squandered
most of it grieving over news that,

at least in kind, wasn't news at all.
This larger insult, that we would forget
when programming changed in the fall,
was why I failed to show delight

when the seedlings first broke soil;
it didn't seem to be the miracle
I'd promoted. Of course, to any girl
at one, a garden's no more a miracle

than a bowl of ice cream or a straw
in a glass of lemonade, so it's unlikely
there was harm, but I had expected to walk
once through the fields of immaturity,

free of the old, impossible hope
that some goddess or angel or spell
would deliver each missing child home
and the rest of us back out of hell.

China II

At first it was a void from which the key people had come.
Then it was an underworld from which few ascended,
And then it was a land of burning cities from which
Sons could not carry their fathers.

The terraced earth had a life only in photo essays,
Later in films. I did not know it was being shaped
By visionaries who had everything wrong,
Nor that the shape had been drawn by my own cramped vision.

Many around me preferred garden photography to real gardens.
We got along fine; we spoke only good. I never expected to walk
Into a garden eventually, or to find it full of wasps,
Or myself at a loss to describe the animals, or the sound of the water.

Foreign Languages

I learned too late: if you want one to cherish
and comfort you, to be there at times
of near-speechlessness, you have to marry it,

preferably early, before you know the future
isn't yours to give. Marrying later,
when experience has made you wiser,

has perks, but togetherness won't come naturally.
Don't make my mistake. I've had my fun
but ended up with nothing but history.

The first one I experienced out loud
was French, so brief and I so young
that it never got its tongue in my mouth.

Longer was my passion for Latin, bookish
devotion of my teenage years
I once thought I'd spend my life with,

but just as things were getting serious,
along came Chinese, well-read, older,
a painter and poet in one, and top this:

my parents liked him. While technically
there had been others, you could call
this one the first I slept with. Eventually,

though, craving my own identity,
I grew up and left. Both of us wept.
But it wasn't long before an equally

exotic arrival, Japanese, seduced me.
I loved the unembarrassed pleasure
it took in my neglected femininity,

understanding every hint, evasion,
unfinished sentence… Japanese softened
my voice, style, even ambitions,

but then I ran out of tuition money
and lived austerely with that dullard
English, for years. Oh, there were plenty

of kisses, notably German and Spanish,
and one impassioned summer with Italian;
I also wished for French to return in some lavish

incarnation, like seaside travel or a stranger
with a charming accent, but by now
I knew that when it came to languages,

I was only a flirt or a fling, a girl you date
for fun before you get ready to settle.
And it was all my fault: I couldn't commit

to just one. I loved to take new vocabularies
into my mouth, to accustom my lips
to the unfamiliar, to hear them accidentally

append a *mafan ni* or *kudasai*
to a request for tea or somebody's hand;
was thrilled to discover I didn't know why

the modifier was right, only that the one
that felt right *was*; relished acquiring
the novel syntax, slang, and idiom

by which the next one lived, and quickly
moving in. It's true my resumé suggests
repeated failure, even superficiality,

but it also delivers me back to the day
in first-year Latin when the teacher
gave the origin of *ardent* (from *ardere*,

to burn), and one of the cockier boys yelled,
"Mrs. Swinson, is your husband ardent?"
Instead of getting mad, she only smiled

a wicked smile of knowing joy and said,
"Of course!" For once, she didn't go on.
Never having believed that Latin wasn't dead,

that it was the heart and soul of the Romance
languages, I caught my breath – no, *its* breath,
the breath of the written word as its silence

uncoiled into understated passion. Right here,
in the cinderblock room, chalk-clouded,
fixing our ablatives, was not so much a teacher

as a woman, alive and doomed as the rest of us.
I converted then, for better or worse, to a lifetime
of beginnings. To the romance of languages.

College

I thought the point was breadth
And put off depth.

That's how I ended up twenty-one
And wedded to none.

Some say that's ideal.
But we're nothing without a field.

Even if you later defect,
It counts to have been obsessed.

Geography

Every time I return to the neighborhood,
I've come from a different place.
I'm beginning to know my tendency:

The level I seek is not in a high-rise
But I like to walk, so rural routes are out,
And while the outskirts of town feel like home to me,

They also seem the periphery—
Where I wait for the bus at seven each morning,
Try to memorize the history of Europe,

Learn to drive, and start to know consequences.
The outskirts are where I work toward the center,
Which is not necessarily the heart of town

Or a brilliant career or seeing all the year's films.
But sometimes it asks for acquaintance with landmarks
Or at least a passing knowledge of the stars.

And some nights, even in the absence of clouds,
All constellations refuse to be traced
And the way to their points is in not looking up.

Ars Longa

Always partially stranded
on the newly founded island
of you and me, I'm unwitting
queen of a miniature nation
where life is warmth, sleep, and nursing,
and art merely reflection.

You make your syllables one by one,
filling our streets with citizens.
We aren't born languageless at all.
Meaning is mostly context;
everything I said before is trivial.
At night the only music is your breath,

classical, miraculous, and ordinary.
I could almost live without a dictionary.
Your father and I once tried
to rescue novels from a flood;
today you wouldn't recognize
the two of us, sifting through muck,

laying pages out to dry, engrossed
in plots, oblivious to the most
important book we'd ever write.
But take my word for it: We felt
so sure that *longer than life*
meant *better than life* that we could well

have missed the journey back
(by way of Sam I Am and Jill and Jack).
I know it was never about innocence
—that's adult nostalgia getting it wrong—
but there were years and years when
life was art and life, and both were long.

Sleep When the Baby Sleeps

Experienced mothers advise it, so I will,
as soon as I've picked all the Cheerios
out of the couch and carpet, filled
another vacuum-cleaner bag with Tayto's
fur, wiped the lead dust off the windowsills,
marked the student poems for tomorrow's

workshop, taken 500 milligrams of calcium,
read a *New Yorker* story on the engineering
of the Twin Towers, and created a lesson on
The Rape of Nanking, which makes me weep
for so many women and children and men
that I forget that I'm supposed to sleep

when the baby sleeps. I'll sleep after
I've tied all the bad news up for recycling,
when I've finished the glass of water
I was supposed to drink before nursing,
when I've marveled at the face of the daughter
who hasn't heard the world is full of weeping,

when I can live with rebellion, poverty,
abduction, and execution wrapped in inverted
pyramids and delivered in time for tea,
and sleep, so to speak, like a baby, who's sure
that every time she departs for the unknown sea
of song and dreaming, her mother won't disappear.

China III

It is too much a part of things,
even though the source is not within.

In small American cities
with and without universities,

it keeps a constant presence
in the Confucian sense,

the inner arriving to match
the outer, spirit not separate

from matter (the latter illusion
left by the missions

the people have made such fine
use of). There are times

when you have to pretend
to embrace an idea or befriend

your adversaries. If constantly
misinterpreted, use the mystery

as currency. You have to start
somewhere. Be wise: depart

from where they've already put you.
A country itself can't betray you.

I Can't Become a Buddhist

because I grew up vaguely Methodist
and most of the Buddhists
I know are men who turned Buddhist

after finding the religion
in a prepubescent
girl serving prawns and chicken

in coconut milk, steamed sticky rice,
papayas, and a massage for the price
of a subway token. Because they drive

cars bearing FREE TIBET bumper stickers
but would let their neighbors wither
and starve. Because they slither

up and down the supermarket aisles
waiting for the chance to ask girls
like me *Where are you really from?* while

stocking up on mung beans and swelling
with the memory of that excellent
backrub in the hands of a thirteen-

year-old goddess who's probably working
for Nike now, if she's working
at all. Because their renouncing

is pointed, because all they ever wanted
was to be different and Buddhism planted
the seed of a new Me in a stunted

self-image. Because they insist on roaming
the city in off-white robes, deflecting
the sun's hot gaze, saffron being

too conspicuous and white being too damned
unprofound and likely to be sandwiched
between red and blue in a crowd of Americans.

Adolescence

The trouble was not about finding acceptance.
Acceptance was available in the depths of the mind
And among like people. The trouble was the look into the canyon
Which had come a long time earlier
And spent many years being forgotten.

The fine garments and rows of strong shoes,
The pantry stocked with good grains and butter—
Everything could be earned by producing right answers.
Answers were important, the canyon said,
But the answers were not the solution.

A glimpse into the future had shown the prairie
On which houses stood sturdily.
The earth was moist and generous, the sunlight benevolent.
The homesteaders dreamed up palaces and descendants,
And the animals slept soundly as stones.

It was a hard-earned heaven, the self-making
Of travelers, and often, out on the plains,
Mirages rose of waterfalls, moose, and rows of fresh-plowed soil,
But nobody stopped to drink the false water.
Real water being plentiful, they were not thirsty.

A few made their fortunes from native beauty,
Others from native strength, but most from knowledge,
As uncertainties in science could be written off to faith.
Faith was religious and ordinary life physical,
And spiritual was a song that had not yet arrived.

Creation

All those months I tried to save sleep
like money, and reread the manuals.
Who did I think I was?

So many before me had never turned back,
surely it was paradise—or a black hole.
When I was seventeen I knew
the fight was for art or nothing,

and while I surely knew *something*,
it wasn't the meaning of *nothing*.
Everyone's mother could have been someone.

Now that it's happened, I no longer fear
my middle name, woman under a roof.
Here on earth, a complete escape from abstraction.
Either you're there or you aren't.

The old selfishness is inconceivable,
the feasts and aimless journeys,
the long baths, the potential lives—

None of it glows next to the enormous eyes,
the twenty fine digits, the miniature
laundry, the library of talking animals.
I'm always hungry now, or my teeth itch,

or all the adults in sight are exhausted,
but labor has never been lighter.
Once upon a time I was a writer

and nothing else, with books in me.
Right. At the first sight of blood
I should have known, this was one load
language couldn't carry.

Publication

The innermost, laid bare on sheets.
Most extreme and mundane dreams
counted and recounted like a president's

indiscretions, for whoever cares to hear.
Once, the effort appeared to be for no one,
or for some particular him or her

who'd guard both message and manner
from any public, however small. It was easy
to say the things you would never utter

in life. Now the persona trails the person
like a lover who won't accept it's over;
no matter how slight or yielding your form,

you can't get out of the tailored dress,
even at home, long after the party.
Nothing will ever be *former* or *ex-*

or fully forgotten. Once, you tried to be
the sort of woman whose life
was the event, not the scrutiny

given it afterwards. All those pages
into the trash—but still you couldn't act
without thinking. So here you are, engaged,

sworn, wedded, too late to change your mind,
to a contrivance you thought was like fiction,
a book you could walk away from anytime.

Fear

From the beginning, they learned not to feel any.
They're usually good people, praised by neighbors,
Quick to shovel snow from the walkways.
They're reliably cheerful, even with telemarketers,
And their houses are clean from Monday to Sunday.

But it's hard to picture them at night, unable to rest,
Sick from the latest on Iraq and Afghanistan.
Name a current war, and they imagine terrorists
And despots, not toddlers who can't understand
That they mustn't cry because everything depends on it.

Ambiguity is all they can't tolerate.
Stories without resolution, abstract portraiture—
Why stir things up for the hell of it?
They're willing to discuss the new counterculture,
Even read a book you suggest, but as they see it,

The past is over. If they were unloved by their mothers
Or shouted into submission at every stage
Of development, they're fully recovered.
If others keep having kids they can't raise
And quitting jobs, it's from lack of resolve, or bad culture.

They're glad to explain their position: We overcame, too.
Our parents used to be poor. One of them was violent.
We were brought up on unspoken racism and junk food
But turned out OK and not racist. Hey, we're resilient.
We triumphed over rocky beginnings. And so can you.

Female Infanticide: A Guide for Mothers
in order of expediency

I
Ultrasound, abortion.

II
Drowning; asphyxiation.

III
Hilltop abandonment.

IV
Automobile accident.

V
Failure to immunize; ill nutrition.

VI
Lack of activity; inattention.

VII
Care by little-known relations.

VIII
A mixup on a family vacation.

IX
Wait until you have a son;
put the female up for adoption.

X
Create a scandal in her adolescence.
Her options: suicide, disappearance.

XI
Raise her as one of her brother's servants;
marry her off at your convenience.

XII
Keep her unwed (use psychological torture).
In old age a daughter is fine good fortune.

From the Provinces

When the space shuttle Columbia broke apart
over the American South,
some thought humankind had asked for it,

that the stars had been put out of reach for a reason.
That we were meant to marvel
from earth, then write poems—or science fiction.

Unwittingly I subscribed to this in high school
when I couldn't conquer physics,
and Saturday morning, turning on the news,

I held our daughter tight before the television sky,
breathed in the toddler-scent,
and considered locking her up for life

in safety and ignorance. I had entertained
the idea before, ten months
into motherhood, when four commercial airplanes

blasted into all our sight. Now the notion
of the families watching
from Cape Canaveral disabled the imagination

again; I thought of those moments en route to the airport
when you can't be certain
whether the person you mean to collect is still airborne

or safely on the ground, and tried to multiply
the unease by a million
but couldn't do the math. How can I keep my

child provincial, I wondered, trying to figure out
how I would explain
her parents' contempt for blockbuster movies, corporate

logos on everything, multicultural cliché.
I'd have to tell her Gandhi
and MLK Jr. should have played it safe

and not incited peace, that those who knowingly ran
into the burning towers
to usher strangers out should never have given

their breath. I'd have to urge her not to travel
to developing regions,
not to raise her hand too often, not to read novels

that expose the anguish of being a woman
or a man. Of course she'd rebel.
And it isn't what I want, although I understand

why the father of one astronaut told the press
he'd rather have his son
unknown and alive than a hero and dead.

Children subvert your discoveries; they wake
at night in search
of affirmation, and make the parents hesitate,

now that aloneness—the original national
illusion—is gone,
before everything they once regarded as trivial.

Crossing the street. Opening mail. Choosing shoes.
Piling the bountiful groceries
into a cart. Waking up, turning on the news.

Spring

It's not because of the brevity of blossoms
or the fevers of pollen.

It's not that I want twelve months of cold
or that I never got enough fire or snow.

Spring once signaled the emptiness of summer,
red season I was born to, under

the balmy sun that lights the literature,
the stolid architecture...

But I'd prefer emptiness all year
and spring refuses it, filling the ear

with song and the finest powders,
opening shells and peeling the layers

winter made of ice and wool.
The first breeze against the skin is cool,

soon to be followed by midday's
burning, swims in blue bays,

fear of love's passing,
and the chance of forgetting

to drink light and water
for descent into winter.

Spring is all about death.
I unfold each cotton dress,

its colors fainter than I remember,
and know it's going to disappear

again to the attic, and I'll drive
once again down those divided

highways, promising change.
At the light, there is no evading

the toll: Under guise of sunny
afternoon, spring takes all your money.

Provincetown

All winter, it is so enormous, you forget you're there,
yet so small you are unmistakable in it,
a classical figure halfway up a mountain.

Every morning is another riff on exile,
not miserable like Ovid's, but lonely like the cities
of adolescence, in which you keep getting lost

on the way to your life. Decades and miles
go out with the tide. You're back, turning down bargains,
locking keys in the house, mistaking beauty for love.

It begins to feel like a future, perpetually imminent.
Since you learned to drive, money's been pouring
out of your purse, while dogwoods like open hands

go unnoticed, azaleas on fire, white sun on pavement.
Someday you'll drive a worse car than your immigrant parents
ever had to be seen in, to pull up on this bar of sand

just so you might return to that unremarkable place
with the knowledge you wish you'd possessed
while surrounded by the hot-pink fragrance

of southern spring, tart fruit fallen from branches,
those mysterious, dark-haired people from nowhere
whose arms encircled you, then sent you on your way.

Things Chinese

Once, I tried to banish them all from my writing.
This was America, after all, where everyone's at liberty
To remake her person, her place, or her poetry,

And I lived in a town a long way from everything—
Where discussions of "diversity"
Centered mainly on sexuality.

My policy, born of exhaustion with talk about race
And the quintessentially American wish for antecedents,
Eliminated most of my family, starting with the grandparents,

Two of whom stayed Chinese to their final days,
Two of whom were all but defined by their expertise
On the food of the country I was trying to excise.

It canceled out the expensive center
Of an intense undergraduate curriculum
And excluded the only foreign language I could talk in.

It wiped out my parents' earliest years
And converted them to 1950s Georgians
Who'd always attended church and school, like anyone.

My father had never paused at two water fountains
And asked a white man which he should drink from,
And never told his children what the answer had been.

My mother had never arranged a migration,
Solo at seventeen, from Taipei to wherever,
But had simply appeared in Gainesville out of ether,

And nothing about their original languages
Had brought them together. Their children
Had never needed to explain to anyone

Why distinctness and mystery were not advantages
When they were not optional, and never wondered
If particular features had caused particular failures.

For months I couldn't write anything decent
Because banned information kept trying to enter
Like bungled idioms in the speech of a foreigner.

I was my own totalitarian government,
An HMO that wouldn't pay for a specialist,
And I was the dissident or patient who perished.

The hope was to transcend the profanity of being
Through the dissolution of description and story,
Which I thought might turn out to be secondary

To a semi-mystical state of unseeing,
But everywhere I went there was circumstance,
All of it strangely tainted by my very presence.

Asian Driver: The Sestina

It's an expression you're not supposed to use,
like "black basketball player" or "fat person,"
unless you are a member of the group,
in which case you can even tell jokes.
Did you hear about the Asian driver
who stopped at the red light?

Actually, no one should use the phrase lightly.
Head for the road after using it,
and you'll probably be hit by an Asian driver.
It's plain hubris, unless you are a person
of Asian descent, in which case the joke,
in spite of being on your I-group,

might get you blamed, thanks to group
affiliation, regardless of who ran the light;
such is the power of the joke.
Most of my life, I never heard anyone use
the expression, but I am only the person
I am. Remarks about Asian drivers

probably stopped when I, possibly a driver
and certainly Asian, joined the group.
For years I believed that every person
would be judged on the heeding of lights
and signposts, that racial profiling was used
solely in the hot pursuit of thieves. Jokes

were trivial. Besides, the only jokes
I'd ever heard concerning drivers

were the criticisms men and women used
against each other (women, as a group,
were said to slam on brakes at yellow lights;
men sped up; both would harm the person

in the crosswalk). Later, I became a person
who wrote textbooks. The boss banned jokes
about stupid people, Asian drivers, etc. A light
went on: "Asian" was a kind of driver!
When I parallel-parked badly, it had group
repercussions, same as when I played piano or used

a calculator. I always try not to take it personally,
but it's hard to regroup when you've gotten the joke
too late, like a first-time driver running a light.

Asian Driver: The Haiku

If poets don't drive,
and women can't, nor Asians,
how will I get home?

Postpartum Vocabulary

Offspring: a misnomer; they do not
spring *off* you so much as *upon*

you, quaffing your very blood
long after the umbilicus wraps up

its effort, long after the initial bath
and swaddling in bunnied terrycloth.

Prolactin: best drug you ever took,
invisible, balsamic as milk.

Birth: deceptive term primarily
pertaining to young but equally

applicable to old: wholesale reordering
of body and thought; amazement at former

existence, which now looks absurd.
Hunger: once, inconvenience answered

by sandwich; now, urgent condition
signaled by screaming (young) or sensation

of imminent collapse (old); occurs
for both every one to three hours.

Maternity: adj. describing garments
appliquéd with balloons and / or kittens,

or leave from work in exchange for more
relentless work than anyone ever paid you for;

n., inability to sleep accompanied
by inability to wake, both accompanied

by elation, excess laundry, and renewed
incomprehension of cruelty.

Solitude: once, being the only person
in the room; now, the illusion that no one

is calling your name, which, regardless
of origin, is all about whose mother you are.

The First Trimester

Since you haven't told and look the same,
there's plenty of time to adapt to the changes.

Nobody holds open doors. Subway riders
gaze deeply into the face of Ann Landers.

The driver who edges you out in the parking lot
does it again, unashamed, at the checkout.

Bring something back to Customer Service
and get glowered at, a fish your only witness.

Inquire about uncooked eggs in the Caesar
salad, uncoiling the waiter's covert anger.

With drinking pals, order juice or Evian;
prepare to be seen as a budding Puritan.

Before the belly arrives to explain itself,
you have to appear to look out for yourself,

which nobody likes, so when snaps and buttons
begin to resist, you're ready and willing to fatten.

Woman under a Roof

I've long resisted the roof
in my Chinese name, *An*,
for peaceful, tranquil, safe.

Vying with men as if I were
a peer, I flirted with the language
but considered it backward

like the PRC: live chickens hung
by the feet, spies in the courtyard,
fatal gossip, justice for none.

And if names determine lives,
I must have gone to Harvard
to be a more exciting wife;

if I held fast to the liberty
my diligence had bought,
if I claimed my body

was not the map of my future,
if I dared leave my children
under another's roof, there'd be war.

So this is it, in middle America.
Most days, it feels the same as peace.
Most days are dull, without trauma,

and every autumn, girls still splendid
in denim and strawberry lip gloss,
smart as foxes and nearly as quick,

claim to hold sacred the task
of nourishment, claim to be creatures
that must be supported, just as a calf

whose flesh will sate the hunger
of the men who raise it is supported:
tenderly, so the results will be tender.

Early Work

Sometimes I think it is too accessible.
Other times, even I have no access to it at all.

It recedes like the glove I lost on the beach, in rain
and cold, and didn't miss until the tide had come in.

At times I can push myself back into the music,
but there are too many reasons not to go back.

That night, the dog and I returned to the beach to look.
The tide, nearing the houses, left little room to walk.

The only music in the air was classical,
composed by neither human nor animal.

The dog's damp nose twitched at everything
as she traveled not in search of anything.

Only one of us was fool enough
to search the vanishing beach for a glove

as if the ocean could choose what to swallow.
While the dog made loops in the sand and shallows,

my hand could not remember what it was to be warm.
At last we gave up, and followed our own tracks home.

Secundigravida

A road I've walked before, familiar
in its novelty, a trail at once irregular
and kind, it's become an adventure

to be assessed in the past imperfect,
no longer the singular event, specific
only to itself – so I can just about admit

that it might be the last. Prudence
forbids cajoling for more abundance
from the gods, yet I'm also reluctant

to declare satisfaction, as there's little
they abhor more fiercely in mortals
than complacency. Therefore I'm careful

to mourn as well, to let go the glorious
moment of finding out, the profuseness
of the middle trimester, the epic sense

of arrival in the third, and concentrate
instead on sore feet and stomachaches,
blotchiness, fatigue, the awkward gait,

forbidden food and drink, unwanted
vastness. Still, an unacknowledged
happiness will show. One's sorely tempted

to accept the last of the blackberry pie,
to kiss maternal sacrifice goodbye,
to confess that something is divine

about the work in progress, and take
her chances with celestial rage.
Were it practical in our current state,

we'd be besides ourselves aloft this second
fleeting peak in the forward composition
of our lives: one, two, one, two, one.

Anxiety

My freedom is double-edged,
the grief edge leaping back
to get me in the wrist every time.

My mind is full of ambitions,
but in the end I am all mother,
with choices, guilt or depletion.

It's fall, season in which my daughters
arrived, season of the only true promises,
when the cruelty of flowers abates,

but all I can think of is the pledge
I made when I allowed this to happen.
How hollow my word has become,

how mean and tragic I've become,
how poor a provider, weak in skeleton
and spirit. The milk that always comes

is my bones, and when it's in a bottle,
the baby wants none of it. My arms
are in demand. All they hold is my head.

With Children

As it turns out, there was never a time
when they were not already with you.

Nor were you free of the parent
deep in the body, before the mind got word.

They snuff out each ungratefulness
by crushing the leisure that made it;

no dreaminess is match for a tower
of blocks and its moat of applesauce

on the oriental rug. The written word
cannot compete with milk or tears;

the spoken word can sometimes make
a deal, but rhetoric by and large

yields nothing. Elmo is there, or he isn't.
The pizza is, or is not, littered with olives.

Between expeditions to the superstore,
the park, and that abstraction called work,

there's never enough time together,
never enough alone. Never enough—

it's how you felt about other things
you craved, before you imagined

that you would want this one so badly.
And now there's less of more than ever.

The Girls Learn to Levitate

At last, they are not girls.
They were not born to a house of wailing.
The housekeeper, who owns one pair of shoes, did not pity them.

As the sun sinks, they no longer inhabit their bodies.
Their bodies did not inhabit their mother's body.
Their mother did not waste her blood.

They are lighter, lighter;
they did not fail at suicide.
Little souls escaping, they drift to the ceiling like steam.

From above, they watch the bodies
pour cups of tea, eat pork dumplings,
fold and refold lace napkins.

They watch the boys push the bodies around;
they watch the parents plot their fates:
a profitable marriage, a caretaker in age.

Although the bodies protest, the girls feel nothing.
Out on the balcony, concentrating on the release
of earthly burdens, they rise unsteadily to the orange sky.

ADRIENNE SU was born in Atlanta in 1967, and grew up there. She went to Harvard College (Cambridge, MA), where she got her A.B. in 1989, and the University of Virginia (Charlottesville, VA), where she received an M.F.A. in poetry in 1993. In 1993-94 she was a writing fellow at the Fine Arts Work Center in Provincetown, and in 1995 was the first Ralph Samuel Poetry Fellow at Dartmouth College (Hanover, NH). For a number of years she worked as a freelance writer and editor for educational publishers such as Scholastic. A dedicated home cook, she has published essays on cooking in magazines such as *Saveur, Prairie Schooner, Beard House,* and *The NuyorAsian Anthology*. Adrienne's poetry awards include a Pushcart Prize and a Reader's Choice Award from *Prairie Schooner*. She has done residencies at Yaddo and the MacDowell Colony, and in 2003 was the resident poet at the Frost Place in Franconia, NH. Adrienne teaches at Dickinson College in Carlisle, PA, where she is poet-in-residence; among her courses are poetry workshops, Asian-American literature, contemporary American poetry, and a course on writing about food and culture.

The author would like to thank the Corporation of Yaddo, the Frost Place in Franconia, New Hampshire, and Dickinson College for grants of time and space that made these poems possible.

And for their vision concerning poems in progress, gratitude to Darrach Dolan, John Meredith Hill, Cynthia Huntington, Jennifer Joseph, Cleopatra Mathis, Sharon O'Brien, April Ossmann, Faith Shearin, Melanie Sumner, and Cedric Yamanaka; and for related sustenance, to Jennifer, Kendall, and Jonathan Su, and Paula Fagerberg Volovoi.